WHO LET THE CRABS OUT?

Navigating the Waters of Life

J. BLACKWELL GORDON

Copyright © 2019 by J. Blackwell Gordon

Published by KWE Publishing, www.kwepub.com

ISBN: 978-1-950306-19-0 (paperback) 978-1-950306-18-3 (ebook)

Library of Congress Control Number: 2019920382

All rights reserved.

No part of this book may be reproduced in any form or by any electronic or mechanical means, including information storage and retrieval systems, without written permission from the author, except for the use of brief quotations in a book review.

Acknowledgments

Two books in 1978 inspired the writing this book.

Bach, Richard, *Illusions, The Adventures of a Reluctant Messiah,* Gardners Books, April 30, 2001.

Millman, Dan, *Way of the Peaceful Warrior: A Book That Changes Lives,* HJ Kramer - New World Library; 20th Anniversary edition, September 30, 2000.

Both books told interesting stories. Both books had life lessons within.

My buddy Bill Stainton taught the way to build the stories.

The love of my life Alison Gordon has always supported my dreams. Her additional suggestions guided some of these chapters.

Special thanks to my virtual assistant Nancy Lynch in Round Rock, Texas. Her ability to take my hand written pages and turn them into readable pages will always be appreciated.

Barbara McNichol is a great editor in Tucson, Arizona. Thank you, Barbara for expanding my vision.

Mill Creek became a wonderful part of my teenage years.

In loving memory of my mother Anna Blackwell Gordon and my dad Pomeroy Gordon; I treasure and honor both of you.

Contents

1. Who Let The Crabs Out? — 1
2. Up the Creek with a Paddle — 5
3. Pipe Dreams — 7
4. The Great Disappearing Act — 13
5. Gascony and the Gunboat — 17
   Ocean Dawn — 19
6. The Slow Boat from Fredericksburg — 21
   My Small Craft — 25
7. Roller Coaster Seas — 27
8. Triple Whammy — 31
9. A Flippin' Cold Day — 37
   March — 41
10. Ghost on the Flying Bridge — 43
11. On the Trail of Thunderstorms — 49
12. Clover Dale Creek — 55

My Mistress the Sea — 59
Notes — 61

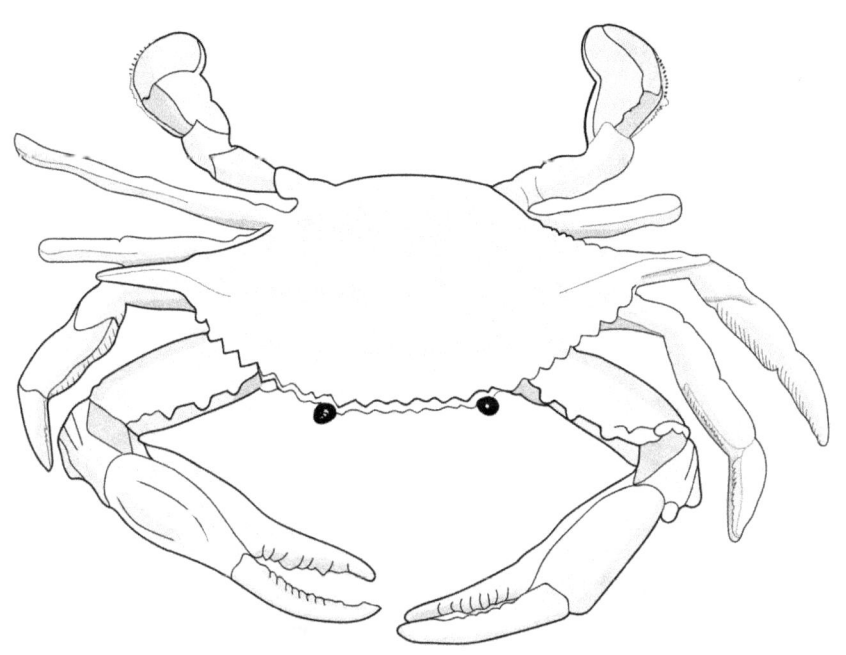

ONE

Who Let The Crabs Out?

Summer days on the front shore were frequently spent fishing in a Chesapeake Bay skiff. The flat bottom boat was easy to row out to the oyster stakes.

Bottom fishing with cut peeler crabs is the preferred bait. Both Mom and Dad enjoyed catching a wide variety of fish – Gray Trout, Croaker (Hard Heads), Spot and Flounder. Not only did the fish like the peeler bait . . . but also the Hard-Shell Jimmy Crabs.

Crabs pulled differently on the line – slow and steady as if walking away with the bait. If you reeled in slowly, the crab could be seen eating below the water level. A quick swoop of a crab net added another one to the wooden bushel basket.

Crabs are strange and unusual creatures – especially to a small boy. Beady eyes, shifting mouth side-to-side: all very interesting to a young boy.

"I'll get a closer look," he thought.

Leaning over into the basket provided a better view.

In a flash, a large Jimmy Crab grabbed the boy's nose. PAIN!

His nose was bleeding from the powerful pincher claw. Like a vise grip, this crab wasn't letting go. MORE PAIN!!!

The boy yelled and threw his head back. The crab let go at the height of the arc, sailing through the salt sea air and back into the mud flats of Ingram Bay.

His mother (the ever-present nurse) began attending the bleeding nose. His dad, with a twinkle in his eye, said,

"Who let the crab out?"

That night, during a fitful sleep, the boy heard a voice ask,

"Who let the crabs out? Who? Who? Who? Who-Who?"

The dream continued. His hand reached over to the bushel basket of crabs. Losing his balance, he tilted the edge. Now crabs were crawling all over the bottom of the skiff.

A chorus chanted,

"Who let the crabs out? Who? Who? Who let the crabs out? Who? Who? Who? Who-Who?"

The dream ended with a cold sweat and feelings of great worry.

Every youngster has strange dreams leading to fear.

All people have great survival mechanisms. Fight or Flight can be triggered by strong emotions, such as anger or self-criticism. This reaction hits the adrenal glands and produces stress, passive aggression, and strong emotional spikes. Such events can then produce physical responses, like fainting, panic-attacks, or even life-threatening heart attacks.

To lessen the adverse impact: take long, slow, deep breaths.

After three long, slow, deep breaths, think of a place of perfect peace and tranquility.

When you're experiencing that beautiful place, silently repeat:

- I am a calm, relaxed person.
- My mind and my body are functioning rhythmically.
- I am using my higher centers of communication and love.

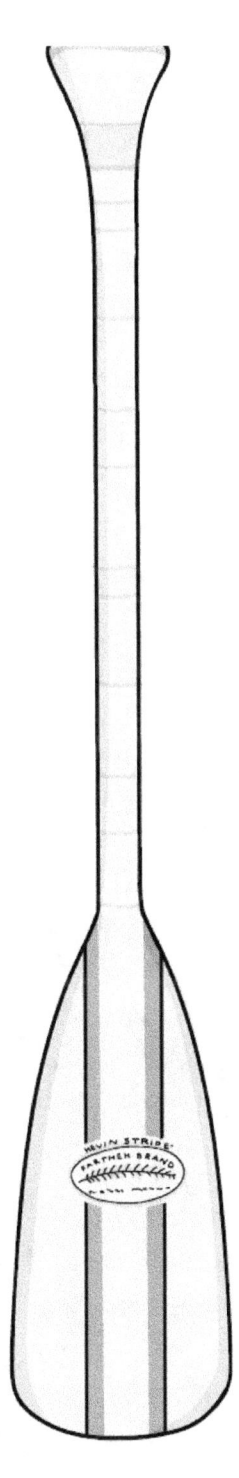

TWO

Up the Creek with a Paddle

A beautiful summer day on the Chesapeake Bay began with two young boys, a green wooden boat, and an idea.

"Why don't we make our own sailboat?" they thought.

Searching their grandfather's barn for materials, they found two abandoned broomsticks – one was just right for a mast, and the other could be the boom. Now, where to find sailcloth? A red sheet of plastic could be cut into a triangular sail.

Cutting a V-shaped notch in the wood transom crafted a paddle into a rudder. Nothing else was needed – right?

The project was declared ship-shape and ready to launch.

First, the boat was eased into Gascony Cove beside the farmhouse dock. Only a few small leaks were a good sign. The red sail was raised and the wind was perfect.

Forty minutes later, with a steady southeast breeze, they rounded Clay Point into Mill Creek. Their starting point lay a mile behind them. The boys were jubilant! Their sailboat was a success!

Now just push the paddle rudder over and head back to the farmhouse.

"Wait a minute! We're not heading the right direction. What's wrong?"

"Why is this boat going backwards?!?!"

As it happens, there is more to sailing than crafting a sail. One needs a centerboard to move against the wind. The boys didn't have one.

They lowered the sail. Taking turns with the rudder-returned-to-paddle, they struggled against the wind.

Three hours later, the exhausted boys flopped down on the sandy shore of the farmhouse.

Although they would become excellent sailors, they never forgot about being up the creek **with** a paddle.

Have you ever been up a creek in your life?

Maybe you turned to go home and found yourself drifting backwards?

The first step is to focus on one small action.

Once you have done that small step, you will feel successful.

From that step, the next step will be shown to you.

Each step reveals itself after you've taken the next step.

As you build on these Stair Steps of Success, you will rise. Your life and your business will grow, by just taking the next step.

THREE

Pipe Dreams

Growing up at the Chesapeake Bay with Uncle Bill was always an adventure. Uncle Bill's dock was littered with the debris of past great ideas gone awry or abandoned in boredom. Now nine, Jasper and his seven-year-old brother, Indiana, lazed around their grandfather's old farmhouse facing the mouth of the Great Wicomico River. They didn't want to miss the next brainstorm. And suddenly, the *big* idea came to Uncle Bill.

Hanging around with his other salty-dog friends at Fairport Marina's local watering hole, Uncle Bill had heard about a big yacht in trouble over at the Fleeton docks across Cockrell's Creek. The next day, he grabbed his faithful young followers and motored over to see this yacht. The yacht was magnificent at sixty-two feet long. Well, okay, maybe it needed a little work.

In fact, the yacht was heeled over on its side at a 45-degree angle. Bill's enthusiasm remained unabated. Not only was he an expert fisherman, he was also a handyman who thought he could fix most anything.

The story Bill related to the boys was that two men from

Washington, D.C. owned the yacht. Washington was not far by water, just up the Potomac River, a tributary of the Chesapeake Bay. The two men were inexperienced at boating and had tied the vessel at Fleeton's marina just because they had gotten that far and no farther. The two men hadn't realized that maintaining a large boat can be very expensive and time-consuming. When the yacht sprang a leak, they weren't around to notice. The only thing holding up the boat was the shallow bottom of Cockrell's Creek under Fleeton's dock.

Taking in the situation as it then stood, Uncle Bill looked around and became very excited to explore this new treasure. And of course, Jasper and Indy were right behind him. The spacious interior left all three very impressed. A large, open area comprised the main cabin and it looked roomy enough to hold quite a few people. A large galley and master cabin would look fabulous, had they not been half-filled with water.

The man and boys walked the deck and examined the condition. They proceeded with an unusual gait, adjusting to the 45-degree angle by carefully crooking one knee and swinging ahead with the other leg. To the boys, it was just like a floating fun house. The boys got giggly and laughed at the comic way each of them oddly edged along.

Bill grew silent and fell into deep thought. Then he announced, "You know guys, I could buy this boat. The owners won't get diddly for it in its poor condition. We'll move it through Ingram Bay to your creek, Mill Creek. I could run it into shallow water and stabilize it with pilings. If I put screen instead of glass in the windows and got the electricity going, I could run a dance hall on it."

Jasper and Indy were struck dumbfounded. They considered the idea and thought it would make a fabulous place to escape from chores. They emphatically/enthusiastically voted, "Yes!"

Jasper and Indy couldn't wait to see the yacht come around into Mill Creek. Every day that summer, they watched off their dock for the arrival of Uncle Bill and the towed yacht.

But the boat never arrived and the boys slowly realized that it never would. The plan had been another one of Uncle Bill's great ideas that would never be. Perhaps money was too short to buy the wreck, or the logistics of becoming buoyant again made moving the yacht too complicated. The boys never heard why.

A hard lesson is to know you can never dream too big, but with the big dream may come disappointment if someone else is making the decisions.

With disappointment come new lessons. Have you ever been frustrated and disillusioned when someone you know and admire doesn't come through for you and your business?

Life is like a journey at sea. You leave from your port with a desired port in mind. Sometimes challenges like strong currents or weather conditions move your ship off course. Does that mean you turn around and start over?

The obvious answer is, "No." You make corrections, plot a new course, and increase speed or modify direction to ease the waves. Your destination remains. Your adjustments help to bring that desired dream.

The first step is for you to recognize that people will be people. That means unpredictability. So where can you turn?

1. The answer is to upgrade your needs to preferences. Instead of thinking, "I really need this to happen," switch your thinking to, "I would **prefer** this to happen." Then, if it doesn't happen, your emotions won't overwhelm you.
2. Realize the truth about from where your real power comes. Power comes from inside, not outside. When fully grounded, you feel a calm force inside. That force is the *I Am That I Am*.

What a thrill when you reach that port! There the sun warms your skin and the light breeze produces the perfect temperature you desire.

Now you know whatever it took was worth it.

There is a new self confidence that arises within you.

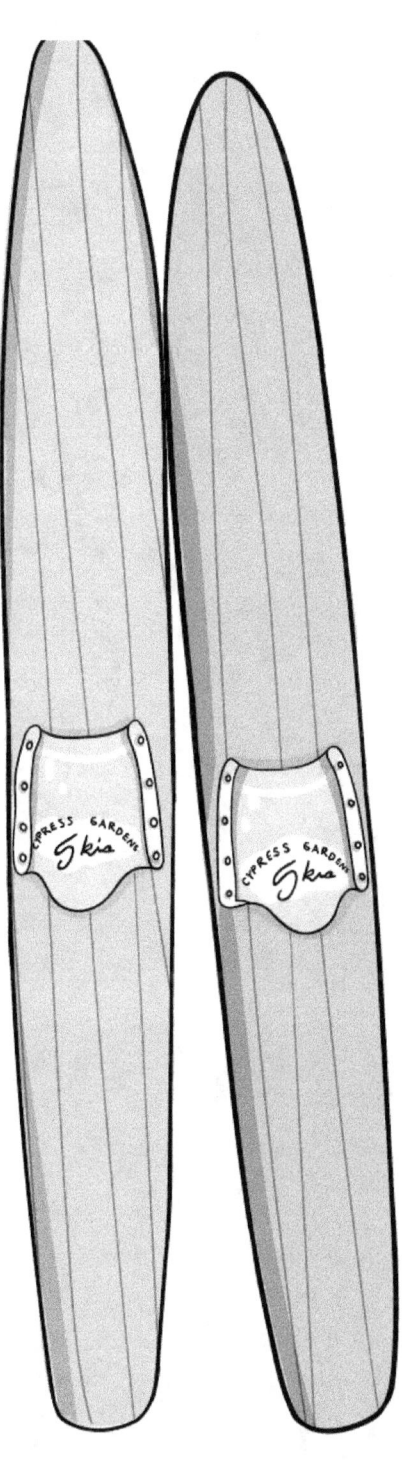

FOUR

The Great Disappearing Act

Hanging out on the farmhouse dock on Gascony Cove was a wonderful way to pass the time. The view of Mervin's Beach and Ingram Bay was very peaceful. Many days were enjoyed swimming on Mervin Christopher's white sand with six feet of water. A makeshift diving board provided hours of entertainment (provided the stinging nettles weren't around).

One Saturday afternoon, the two boys ventured back to their grandfather's dock. They walked the short distance from the Victorian farmhouse (typical Northern Neck style) as the sun warmed their arms.

Across Gascony Cove, a small house was the weekend get-away for the Pendergrass family. Although the cove was small, they had an aluminum, flat-bottomed boat (commonly known as a Jon Boat) with a small outboard motor.

That afternoon, the Pendergrass family gathered on their very short dock for water skiing.

Uncle Bill had a runabout with a twenty-five horsepower outboard for water skiing. Jasper and Indy would ride "shotgun" and knew how much power it took to bring a skier up out of the water.

Much to their surprise, a lone skier's towline was tied to one corner of the Jon Boat's stern. Amazingly, the boat with the skier got up on a plane completing a lazy turn around the cove.

Around again came the boat and skier. This time the boat and skier turned in the same direction. In a flash, the boat flipped over!

The boat, towline, and skier vanished without a ripple!

No sound. No debris. Nothing.

The boys looked at each other in disbelief.

How could a boat disappear like that?

In what seemed a long time, the gas can shot to the surface like a cork. The laughing face of Joe Pendergrass popped up next. He held up his dripping shoes to show that he was okay.

The skier bobbed up last. He seemed to be in satisfactory condition.

What a strange sight! One minute, everyone was enjoying an afternoon ski outing. The next minute, all vanished beneath the waters of the Gascony Cove Triangle!

"This life is a test-it is only a test.
If it had been an actual life, you would have received further instructions on where to go and what to do.
Remember, this life is only a test."
— Jack Kornfield[1]

Although this quote brings smiles, it illustrates the point well.

Growth is the major game in Life.

You are the Star in your own movie. You draw players to act out different roles in your movie. [2]

You are also the script-writer. Behind you and unseen is your

Director. That Director is known by many names. It is the Highest Source of the Universe – God.

Write a letter to your Director. Be very clear and precise about what you desire.

Close your letter with "All this or something even better".

Then let go. Allow your Director.

FIVE

Gascony and the Gunboat

Mother loved history, especially family history. While she grew up on the farm, her Aunt Rose lived in Gascony with a commanding a view of Gascony Cove, Ingram Bay and the Chesapeake Bay.

In 1848, one of the Harding relatives built Gascony on the original foundations.[1] Aunt Rose lived there from 1861 to her death in 1947.

During the Civil War, the men left to fight – some in the cavalry, some in the infantry. The women had to manage the home and the fields.

Pending news of Yankees patrolling the shores of the Chesapeake caused panic. All the silver was buried without a trace. (The silver still awaits discovery/remains hidden.)

One fateful day, the Yankee Gunboat rowed into Gascony Cove. The men searched Gascony for anything of value.

One man found a Masonic pin and brought it to the Captain.

The Captain happened to be a Mason. After one look at the potential treasure, he ordered all loot returned to Gascony. Returning to the Gunboat, they slipped silently out of Gascony Cove.

∼

The ties between human beings cross over the boundaries of war.

Amazing men and women founded our country. George Washington, Thomas Jefferson, James Madison and James Monroe were all Virginians. Their vision excelled by seeing more possibilities.

Imagine traveling by ships, boats and horseback. Boats moved through the rivers allowing exploration throughout Tidewater.

Following animal paths and Indian trails, horseback travel stretched all the way to the Blue Ridge Mountains.

George Washington as a surveyor journeyed following the James River into the Shenandoah Valley. His vision was a System of Locks from the fall line (Richmond area) through the Blue Ridge.

What is your vision?

Do you see beyond your immediate circumstances?

The basis for vision is intuition.

Everyone has experienced some form of intuition, such as knowing someone is about to call.

Intuition can be strengthened. Most prevalent after peaceful sleep or during quiet time, deep breathing can calm busy thoughts. Intuition and inspiration can occur during a warm shower or a relaxing drive.

Long slow deep breaths provide more oxygen to the brain.

By shutting down the daily chatter, new ideas fill and create new space.

Your mind becomes open to receive information and guidance.

Ocean Dawn

Pink skies whispered

before the red sun

spread the majesty

on all looked upon.

A gray freighter

silently gave way

as charter boats

began a new day.

I basked in the glow

feeling the flow

wishing to share this great show

with a special someone I know.

SIX

The Slow Boat from Fredericksburg

What an adventure for the two brothers, Jasper and Indy, now sixteen and fourteen years old – their first train trip! As they boarded the RF&P in Richmond, their mother watched with tears as they departed to their Uncle Bill's home next to the Fredericksburg Battlefield.

Their task for that week was the exterior of Uncle Bill's eighteen-foot runabout Sugarfoot II. Decks showing their weathered age needed sanding and new varnish. When completed, the boat would be ready for another season on the Chesapeake Bay.

After days of breathing sawdust and fumes in the one-car garage, the decking gleamed again and was ready to be launched.

On a hot, Friday afternoon, the boat was carefully trailered to the Fredericksburg City Boat Ramp. The Sugarfoot's decks looked grand. Leaving the older brother in charge, Uncle Bill took the younger one for some additional marine supplies.

Hours passed. Then at 6:00 in the evening, Uncle Bill returned with a question, "Are you ready?"

It was difficult to imagine for what they needed to be ready.

. . .

As he cranked the twin Evinrude 30 horsepower outboard motors, it became clear. He wanted to make the run down the Rappahannock River. The boys quickly handled the dock lines.

From Fredericksburg to Tappahannock, the river meanders dramatically. This beautiful coastal river switches back making wide loops.

As the daylight began to fade, scudding dark clouds of rain moved in quickly. The whole sky broke into sheets of blinding, cold rain.

Continuing downstream, the river opened up at Port Royal. In the dark, they plowed forward in the middle of the river. The twin engines began kicking up mud!!

Visibility was so bad that Uncle Bill grabbed his searchlight. Fourteen-year-old Indy manned the wheel as his older brother grabbed the charts. It would take all three of them to navigate this river in the blowing rain.

Finding the channel was not the only obstacle. Fish stakes (for gill nets) crisscrossing worsened. For two hours, they struggled. Uncle Bill shouted, "Fish stakes!" causing last second adjustments each time. A new chart location was required to find the channel. They kept silent except to call out safe routes.

Finally, they spotted the Tappahannock Bridge. Soon, the boat slowed into a narrow channel on the starboard side, heading for a local marina. Three soaked, storm-worn sailors tied up Sugarfoot II for the night (only halfway to their desired home dock).

After nightmares and cries of, "Fish stakes!" during the remaining night, the next day dawned bright and beautiful. A return to the Tappahannock marina with Uncle Bill, Uncle Robert and the boys' father began early for the second leg of the journey. The eldest son, Jasper, ventured along wanting to see the rest of the Rappahannock River.

The ride was steady and easy with small waves. His father casually observed, then queried, "What a pleasant trip. How could you have been so upset last night?"

You've been through a horrible experience. The next day someone questions it as being anything of concern. Have you ever had that happen to you?

Life is like that. We get thrown a big challenge and then people (family, even best friends) question our experience.

Behind every dark cloud is a silver lining. When we recognize that truth, every challenge is a lesson. Once seen as a lesson, we can learn and grow.

What if we don't want to learn and grow? We don't have to. Whatever we do is okay.

However, we continue to be limited by fear.

The world is not stagnant. The lesson will return.

LESSONS UNLEARNED

REPEAT UNTIL LEARNED.

We can limit our lives by narrowing where we go and what we do. Or we can choose to grow.

So what's holding you back? Would you be willing to take the first steps to grow?

Come on! Let's live life to the fullest!

The horizons are just beginning to expand. You will live in the glow and beauty of a richer life.

My Small Craft

Where once was blue sky and clear water

my small craft dips and sways.

Love can be a gentle summer breeze

or a tempest with gale-force winds.

And now, my mistress, the sea

Weeps for my confused state.

It is not rain that lulls one to sleep

But rather a dark cloudburst of emotion,

and I wonder...

will I ever see the sunshine again?

SEVEN

Roller Coaster Seas

Many a day, the teenager spent saltwater fishing with his uncle. Uncle Bill was an excellent fisherman having been raised on the Chesapeake Bay.

It looked like any other day – sunny with a good wind. They boarded Uncle Bill's open-hulled, eighteen-foot, wooden boat at the old farmhouse dock. With the steady outboard motor humming rhythmically, they slowly pushed out into Ingram Bay.

A couple of big waves protested, but not enough to stop Uncle Bill's fishing for Bluefish. He threw out some chum (Menhaden cut into small pieces) and cast his line over the stern.

Suddenly, the craft began to climb a wave, but not just any wave! As the boat crested the wave, it descended like a roller coaster!

While Uncle Bill was calmly fishing, the teenager's thoughts ran fast,

"That wave is as big as this boat! It must be twenty feet high! The entire boat goes straight up and comes straight down the other side. Oh, no!!! It's doing it again!"

Although Ingram Bay is only about two miles wide, neither shore could be seen. UP DOWN UP DOWN

Then it got worse. His stomach clinched. His gut tried to maintain; however, it was a lost cause. Hanging over the side, his breakfast left his belly and didn't stop. He kept heaving and heaving.

Each wave was relentless, crashing in the same pattern over and over again.

He looked for his uncle. There, stood Uncle Bill, teeth clamped down on a cigar, casting his old fishing rod in search of Bluefish. He seemed to have not a care in the world.

Another wave. Each crest brought another sleigh ride down and back up. Then the young man realized – more dreaded seasickness!

So much embarrassment from being an amateur!

Later, he realized that his uncle was a seasoned waterman, able to handle rough conditions and still pursue his great passion.

What are your passions?

What is it you do better than anyone else?

What would make you stand out in your business?

In the area of service, you could respond faster than your competitors. Whether you choose voice, text or email, you can provide a level of service beyond all others.

If you select written communications, how will that be delivered? There's a postage stamp. That will get there someday. With Priority Mail, your reply has speed and tracking capability. Another option is FedEx overnight.

Whatever they need, whatever they require for the next step, your promptness and attention to detail will automatically elevate your business above the rest.

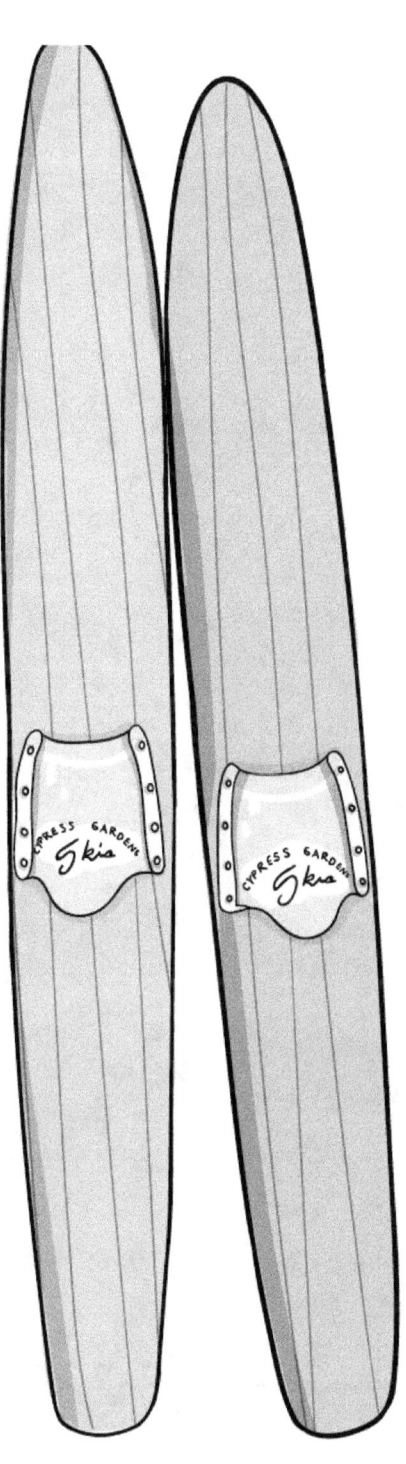

EIGHT

Triple Whammy

Summers on Mill Creek provided a variety of water activities – fishing, crabbing, kayaking, and sailing. The big thrill was water skiing, and not your everyday style of water skiing.

In those days, the best water skiers were in the Cypress Gardens Ski Show. Some of their tricks were amazing. Three skiers jumping a ramp, five skiers carrying flags, twelve skiers forming a pyramid, and many other exciting acts thrilled spectators.

The family loved the water. As teenagers, they learned how to waterski the calm waters of Mill Creek. Almost three miles long and a quarter mile wide, the Creek provided plenty of room for two or three boats pulling skiers.

Everyone developed a specialty. Cousin Camille had a unique ski trick. She and another cousin would get up on two skies. She dropped one ski and placed her foot in his waiting hand. Then releasing her second ski, she would climb onto his shoulders. Two skiers on one set of water skies! Starting to look like Cypress Gardens – Mill Creek style! Then he would drop one ski. Two cousins slalom skiing on one ski – amazing!

One cousin loved jumping with two skis. He stood out by

jumping the boat's wake and clearing his brother's towline. It took good timing and coordination between the brothers. They were proud of their unique trick.

During the middle of the summer skiing season, the younger brother, with his best friend Evan, pulled skiers. Eager to show off his skills, the older brother asked for a tow. Quickly they were off cutting back and forth around the Creek.

The skier loved jumping the wake and building speed on the turns. Speed increased on a 360-degree turn. Driver and skier utilized the centrifugal force beautifully. While the boat driver cut a sharp turn, the skier made the outer circle.

Brave skiers did a double whammy. The boat stayed hard over for two full, 360-degree turns. By the second full circle, the skier was going so fast that the towline could go slack when the boat straightened out.

This particular day, the driver and his buddy decided to give the skier a Triple Whammy – three, full 360-degree turns. The speed on the twin skis surpassed all previous years of skiing. Holding tightly to the tow bar for dear life, the skier's adrenaline was pumping!

When the boat came out and straightened up, the skier saw something strange. The towline was angled between him and the boat. Straining his eyes, realization dawned. The angle was changing, coming closer.

In a flash, there it was! An oyster stake was running down the line and headed right into the skier! There were only two choices: hold onto the towline and run into the barnacled stake or throw away the ski line.

Wisely, taking option two, the skier sank slowly into the warm water. But wait! The skier felt a burning sensation.

Stinging nettles – those dreaded sea creatures from the depths of the Bay! Not just one or two. A whole mass of stinging nettles floated all around.

Pain seared his legs, then his back, stomach and chest! When they pulled him out, his body was covered in swollen, tender welts.

Upon returning to the dock, he inched out of the boat. The usual crowd was watching the skiers that afternoon. Not one of them could look at the red inflamed body of the skier.

Do you ever have something you can't stand to see?

Take a look at your workspace (your desk or whatever space you use).

What does it look like? Is it clean and straight, or does it have clutter – little notes here and there, objects all over it?

If you have asked yourself why you are not productive there, the answer may well be organization.

The easiest way to begin organizing is to create a list.

List only those items needed to be productive.

You now know what items you require.

Clear your workspace of everything except those items.

Use lists in other ways to become more organized.

A daily *To Do* List becomes a check-it-off motivator.

Having this daily list makes decisions easy.

Which item comes next, what are the time constraints and level of importance?

Regular use of lists produces results.

Create a list. Then follow the list.

It's that easy.

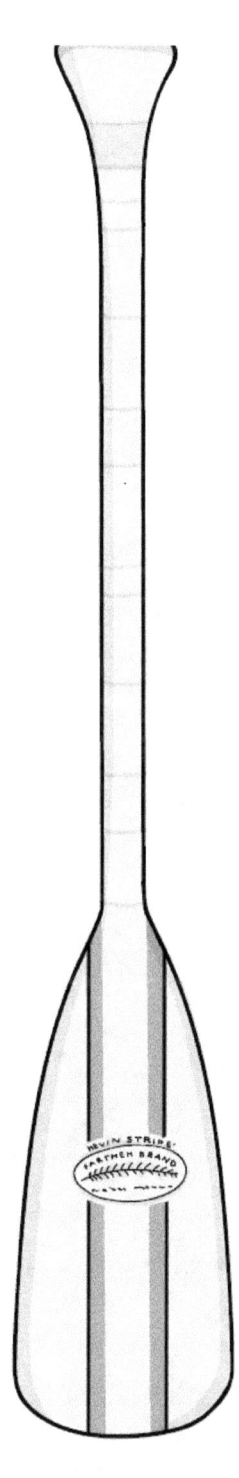

NINE

A Flippin' Cold Day

Feeling the March winds blow on a bright, blustery day can entice a young college student who'd endured a winter vacant of sailing. With the sun streaming down, all thoughts returned to how fun his previous days of sailing have been.

Wonderful memories of sailing Mill Creek and the front shore of Grandfather's farmhouse shaped his thinking. "Why not today?" he asked the wind.

He stared at the old, 1965 eleven-foot Sea Snark sailboat turned over on the shore. Dings on the homemade fiberglass hull reminded him of days sailing through white caps and close encounters with oyster stakes. The beam was only two feet wide. This little craft had seen great days, even though they were long ago (never mind the age of the rigging).

"Let's go," his mind prompted. Turning the hull over and sliding it to the edge of the water, the dagger board, rudder, a paddle, the short aluminum mast, and the lateen sail were moved into their correct positions.

Sail up, pockets emptied, the athletic young man in a red ski parka pushed out from the shore. The blowing wind quickly filled the sail, plunging the small boat rapidly toward the middle of the quarter mile-wide stretch of the creek.

Just as quickly, the wind gusted from a completely different direction. The jibbed sail unexpectedly flew close to his head. Then a tangle in the makeshift mainsheet poly line caught the nylon guide on the boom.

"What the #%!*?"

The sail filled pushing the starboard side down into the water teetering on the edge. BAM!!! The boat capsized into the blue depths chilled from a long winter.

Anger filled his head. "I've been proud to brag that I've never capsized before. This boat's stupid with its simple rigging!"

Righting the boat and sliding his body back inside, he realized that the water was waist-deep. It didn't matter; gaining control did. "I've got to get that sail back up!" was his only thought. Meanwhile, the wind had gusted to twenty miles per hour, shifting the boat from side to side. Finally, he grabbed the boom and held on tight.

Then – wham! The rudder broke off in his hand. Tossing it aside, he quickly scanned his options. Furious, he grabbed the paddle; sticking it under his other armpit attempting to hold it in place was the best he could in this chaos. He hoped the paddle could serve as a substitute rudder. Mere seconds had turned this joy ride into a nightmarish procedure.

"Make it work!" he told himself repeatedly. It was a precarious balance – one hand holding the sail and the other working to keep the paddle in the water.

After struggling to guide the boat back to the waiting shore, he jumped out and hitched a bowline to a nearby tree. Still angry, he heard an approaching motor. His distant older cousin pulled up with a salty remark: "I've been watching you for twenty minutes through my binoculars." This tone was not helping.

Sopping wet and freezing, his mind rambled over the criticism. "Why didn't you come sooner? What were you thinking about while I was floundering?!?!" he demanded of his indifferent relative.

Turning away, he stomped through the field back to the cabin.

Once inside, he felt the cold. With his hands shaking, he couldn't build a fire in the wood stove.

"I've got to get warm."

Pulling one sleeping bag inside another sleeping bag, he slid inside. Feeling very sleepy, he began to doze off.

A thought exploded, "What if I go to sleep and never wake up?!!!"

Jumping up, he left the cabin and squeezed into his faded red Karmann Ghia. The VW heater was known to take forever to heat up. Still shaking, he slowly made it up the hill to his buddy Joey's house.

Joey had a card-playing friend visiting.

Joey said, "Let's go to Tappahannock!"

Inside the truck, the eager, young sailor sat between these two chunky guys. A pint of vodka passed between them. Their body heat did more to warm him than the alcohol.

Later, he found out just how close to death he had been. Hypothermia from being waist-high in frigid water had been dangerous enough. Add alcohol to that, and the body's temperature decreased even more. His friends had actually saved him – with both their body heat and their good-natured laughter after his dangerous adventure.

What's so magical about friends and laughter? Can you remember a horrible situation and a good friend who made you laugh? It cuts the seriousness of the situation in half. It has been proven that the brain triggers an electro-chemical reaction precipitated/triggered by laughter. Yet the real truth lies in the lyrics of this famous Beatles' song, "(I Get By) With A Little Help From My Friends."[1]

In times of pain, retreating inside oneself can produce feelings and thoughts of being lonely. A good buddy or a best friend knows how and when to recount a story to brighten the mood.

That levity causes your mind to switch from brooding to remembering. Thoughts trigger emotions. In this way, laughter is like a starter fluid of emotion added to a small fire of thinking.

Before you can resume brooding, one story leads to another shared funny experience. And the camaraderie increases among trusted friends. So when you and your BFF recount two or more tales, a third person adds to the fun.

An explosion of laughter results as all of you move into the land of merriment.

So, relax whenever you approach the bridge to this land. As if you're in an amusement park anticipating the next ride, enjoy the day. Your soul is restored.

March

March

can be

a cruel mistress.

Her moods

change

so rapidly.

Alluring warmth

gives way

to

bitterness and bite.

But for

those who love her,

her winding path

leads to

Spring.

TEN

Ghost on the Flying Bridge

Living on a forty-three-foot houseboat is an ideal way to enjoy being on the James River. Everything needed is at hand. Peace and tranquility abound.

The cuddy cabin beneath the pilot house feels safe and secure. The double bed provides comfort for sleeping soundly - like it has for hundreds of other restful nights aboard.

But one night, he suddenly woke up from one of those comfortable sleeps as if someone was nudging him, saying, "The engines are starting."

"Go back to sleep," he told himself. But again, the voice spoke, "The engines are starting."

That's when he heard it—a distinctive and familiar sound. "Someone's trying to steal my boat," he fretted. Rapidly, he climbed up to the pilot house. The keys were in starters there. "No one's here. I'll look on the flying bridge," he thought.

Out the pilot house door, around the side deck, he clutched the railing to steady his sleepy steps. Up the ship's ladder to the deck he ascended, then three short steps to the flying bridge. No one was there!

Then the sound came again: the unmistakable starting of the engines. Wait! He did not see any boat keys in place in the ignition. Hair stood up on his neck. "How is this possible?" he wondered. The only answer - a ghost.

Was it the Ghost of Papa Kay, the former owner of that very boat, who long since passed away? Or perhaps his former wife, Eunice? Even though she couldn't swim, she still gave her husband the money to trade in the houseboat to buy a brand new Trojan 44-foot Tri-Cabin Motor Yacht. Or, could it even be the ghost of his previous wife, Janet? She gave Papa Kay the money to buy this houseboat in the first place.

Papa Kay bought six half-gallons every week (five bourbon and one vodka). Since there was always an open bar, his wives (and anyone else) were welcome to drink as much as they wanted. Maybe the method he used had come back to haunt his old houseboat?

He sensed something had to be done right away, so he hurried down the ship's ladder to the engine hatches. Opening the port hatch containing the batteries, he disconnected both of them, thus disabling the starters.

Finally, the night was still and quiet - except for the loud beating of his heart.

His thoughts raced in a fog of drowsiness.

"Maybe with the morning light this will all make sense. Maybe one of the mechanics at the marina could give a reasonable explanation. But right now, I need sleep so I can have a fresh start in the morning."

However, no mechanic could ever explain what happened!

Thankfully, over time, he figured it out. The flying bridge built by Papa Kay had not crowned the floor like a driveway or roadway would. Most likely, rainwater had seeped into the space below and caused a short across the starter wires.

Still, the thought of someone's ghost starting the engines intrigued him.

"Who has come back?" he'd always wonder.

The thick fog on the James River certainly makes ghosts easy to imagine.

Do ghosts from your past trouble you? Do you have haunting memories of events or people? More importantly, are these memories helping or hurting your magnificence? If so, how can you escape from these images that seem so real?

All ghosts have power over you until you let go of the past. If you can release the past with its associated fears in the present moment, you make a powerful shift. You become the Master of your World.

To create this shift, do these four steps:

Step #1: Relax by taking three long slow breaths.

Step #2: Remind yourself that *now* is the only point of power you have. The past is gone and the future is yet to be.

Step #3: Become fully present in the *now*. No distractions, just clarity.

Step #4: Release your fears and let go of everything but the present.

Feel that shift? Repeat these steps until you are fully present in the moment.

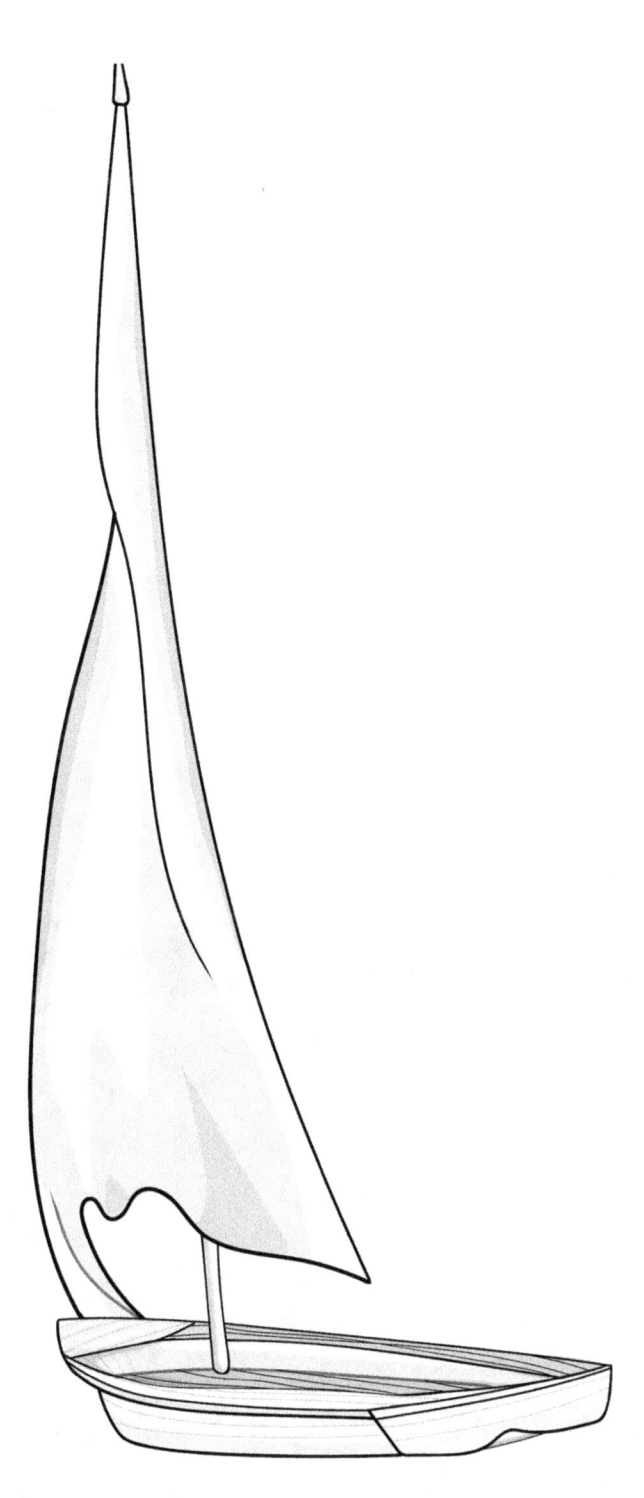

ELEVEN

On the Trail of Thunderstorms

Every competent sailor in the Northern Neck knows to expect thunderstorms almost every hot August afternoon. Occasionally, a large storm develops, but small self-contained storms are normal. When a small one begins to form, the sky is deceptively calm and full of puffy cumulus clouds. Those same beautiful skies can lull the novice sailor into overlooking potential danger.

Four young adults decided it was a great day to test the new, five-meter Boston Whaler Harpoon Sailboat. The breezes seemed steady and the sun was shining.

Tacking against the wind, the new boat ventured forth out of Mill Creek into the much larger Ingram Bay. To the west runs the Great Wicomico River. The only dividing points between Ingram Bay and the Chesapeake Bay are the Great Wicomico Lighthouse (Fleeton Point) to port and Dameron Marsh to starboard. The Chesapeake Bay is twenty-five miles wide east to Onancock on the Eastern Shore.

The small party agreed upon a sail plan south around Dameron Marsh, heading to Windmill Point, a fun destination and good turn-around goal. A full breeze cooled the sailors as the boat clipped along.

Suddenly, an ominous sound rumbled from the mainland as they rounded the Marsh Islands. Thunder definitely bellowed the eerie background noise. Although the sky was still clear directly overhead, fast-moving clouds were coming their way.

One friendly pile of white fluffiness was growing dark underneath. Not a good sign.

Counting the seconds between thunderclaps, the storm began at five miles away and rapidly picked up speed. Four miles, three miles, and then two miles were between the sailboat and the storm.

The proud new boat owner made a quick decision – stop where they were and ride out the storm. With the winds bearing down on them, the route was changing east out into the Chesapeake Bay.

With the rudder turned hard-to-lee, they heaved the anchor overboard and down came the sails.

The first winds blew so strongly that the sailboat with bare mast dragged the anchor. The small crew found themselves moving backward, deeper into the Chesapeake Bay!

All this chaos caused the owner no small amount of shaking and quaking. What had started as a fun idea, had deteriorated into a real, life-threatening situation. Because he initiated the outing, he felt responsible for everyone's safety.

Totally panicked, he asked his skilled sailor buddy, Gary, to take the rudder.

Wise decision! Gary was both a great sailor and fearless friend! Gary took the helm gladly and confidently. Again, they hoisted the anchor. The sails flapped loudly in the wind as they went back up.

The next twenty minutes filled with amazing weather contrasts. To the east, the Chesapeake Bay was clear and sunny. Yet the Harpoon was pursued by dark clouds, lightning, and growing white caps. Beauty promised tranquility ahead while terror threatened to chase them down from behind.

Gary, as newly appointed Captain, made the decision to steer to port and back to Ingram Bay. All on board happily cheered as the thunderstorm continued across the Bay and they sought safety on dry land.

The new owner was exhausted and vowed never to chase thunderstorms again.

Frozen in that moment, panic creates overwhelming thoughts.

The answer is surrender. Surrender paves the way for new paths.

Follow the Thread of Excitement

Here are your next steps:

1. Do whatever excites you.

If something doesn't excite you, do nothing.

2. When you are energized from doing this step, your enthusiasm will change your mindset.

3. Do the next activity that excites you.

This will be whatever holds your interest, gives you strength and renews your energy.

As you continue to immerse yourself in each step, doing just what you love, your path becomes clearer.

If your business is built on these steps, your enjoyment of what you're doing attracts others to you.

They feel your contagious excitement. They feel how alive you are.

It is extremely simple. Just follow what excites you.

Follow the Thread. And only that.

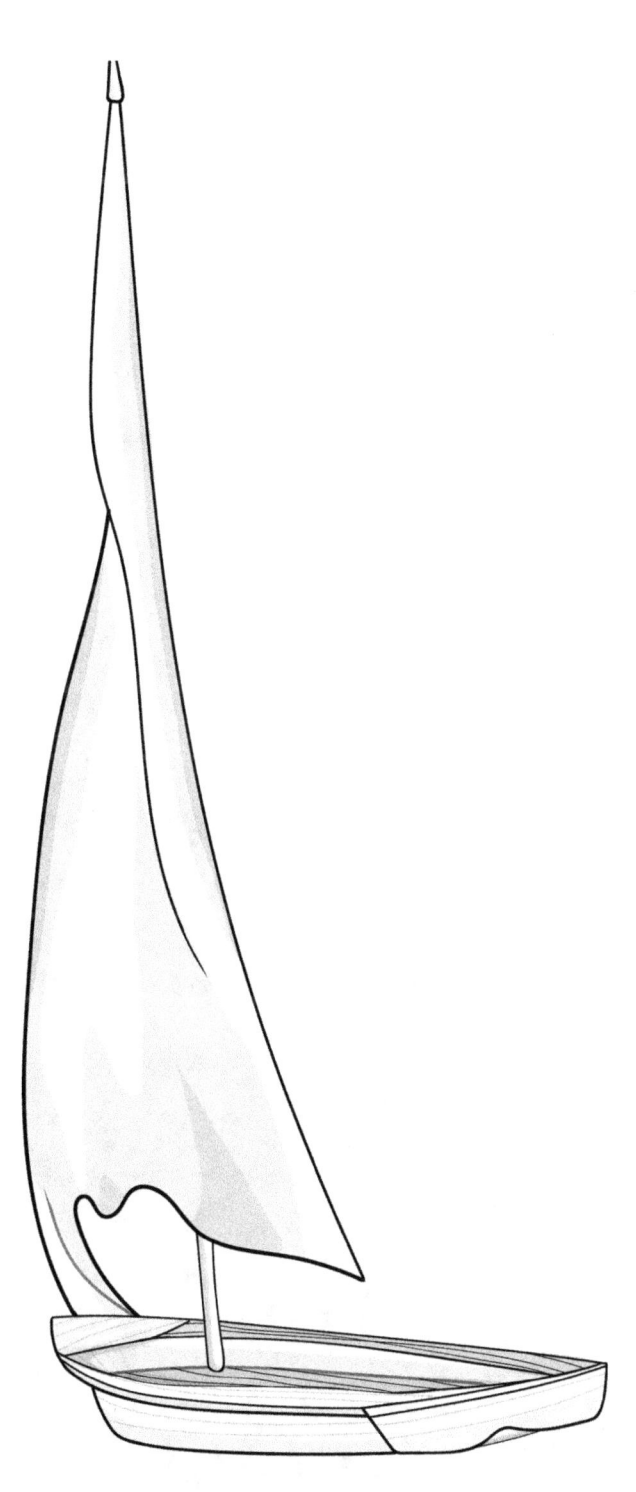

TWELVE

Clover Dale Creek

Perfect sailing days are marked by a constant breeze from one direction, such as wind from the southeast at eighteen miles per hour, and sunny skies. The main and the jib sail can be cleated on each reach.

Jeanne and Jasper set out of Mill Creek and into Ingram Bay. The fair wind made rounding Dameron Marsh easy.

The Marsh is a combination of small islands and shallow waters. Long ago, a sandy island there provided many pleasant memories. An entire family riding in a Chesapeake Bay skiff could enjoy a picnic lunch on the sparkling, white beach.

On an easy reach, the sailors swung wide, clearing the mud flats of Dameron Marsh. Coming up into the wind, they saw Clover Dale Creek once known for Clover Dale (an ante-bellum home).[1] It appealed to their sense of adventure.

A beautiful beach lay beside the creek opening. For further exploration, they brought the 5.2 Whaler Harpoon Sailboat to the shore's edge. Small rocks were present everywhere – very unusual for the bay's known sandy beaches and mud flats.

. . .

Leaving the bow pointed into the wind, both set off to find any potential treasure washed up on high tide. A few sea shells (mostly oyster) were easily found. Unfortunately, no extraordinary finds.

After the short walk, the refreshing breeze called them back. Pushing out from the shore, the main and jib sails were hoisted to continue the enjoyment.

Wait a minute! What was happening with the centerboard?

Try as they might, the centerboard remained up, inside the fiberglass trunk. Repeated efforts were to no avail.

With this wind and nothing to stay their course, the Harpoon was side-slipping rapidly. Dameron Marsh was looming to port.

There were old sea stories about the Marsh. The mosquitoes were reportedly fierce. One story of a man washed up on the marsh shore instilled fear of the immediate attack by these relentless warriors. In desperation, he found a large iron kettle and pulled it over himself. Mosquitoes hungry for fresh blood penetrated the kettle. Using his shoe, he nailed their beaks. The man and the kettle with attached mosquitoes were never found.

Regardless of the old sea story, the shallow mud flats were no place for a sailboat. In an increasingly desperate attempt, they worked rudder back and forth in a sculling motion. It was like a never-ending arm-wrestling match.

Minutes seemed like hours. Off the bow, a small opening between the marsh and the next sand island was the only chance.

With the rudder almost out of the water, they floated over five inches. What a relief! Without escaping that shallow passage, the return to Mill Creek would be impossible.

But wait – with no centerboard active, turning to the port channel was also impossible! Too far to paddle, the direction of the wind was the only option.

On the horizon lay Sandy Point. That would be their new destination. The ride became a little relaxing. Closer and closer, the wind drove the Harpoon forward.

As clearer vision of the shoreline crystalized, the receding waves revealed another danger…

Concrete well curbs sunk for breakwater – their jagged tops would shred the fiberglass hull to ribbons!

The next receding wave revealed a four-foot opening between two of the concrete barriers. With adrenaline pounding and gasps of salt sea air, the rudder became another arm-wrestling challenge!

With a soft sigh against the sand, the hull survived. Everyone was safe and a disaster was averted.

Have you ever had a perfectly beautiful day change with just one glitch? Where were you and what happened?

Did you give up? Or when faced with the circumstances, did you make choices?

In that moment, you made a decision. Whether you know it or not, you made the best decision based on all the information you had.

Wouldn't it be great to have more choices?

Do this exercise. Write down your challenge in Red ink at the top of a blank page.

Number 1 through 10 leaving a blank line between each numbered line.

As you begin, let go of any judgements you have.

The first ones will be obvious.

Push beyond and open up more possibilities.

No matter how silly or even ridiculous, write each thought down.

Remember, you are just gathering alternatives at this point.

When you feel you are drawing a blank, set the paper aside.

Later after a shower, relaxing bath or a short nap, another idea will come. Make sure to make a written note and transfer it to your numbered alternates.

Continue until you have at least seven (preferably ten) alternatives.

Now review your list with your alert mind.
Notice the ones pulling your attention the most.
If you like, prioritize them.
You may be surprised that some new ones attract you.
Pick your **best choice.**
Watch the magic unfold and move forward with zeal and enthusiasm!

My Mistress the Sea

Floating at the mooring
    the gleaming white hull
        shines in the sun-kissed waters.

Her rigging hums
    with stiff afternoon breeze

With infrequent and irregular beats
    the lapping on her hull chants.

The creaking of nearby dock lines
    and the tangy salt sea air
    eases my step.

Once more
    my soul
    has returned
    to my mistress
    the sea.

Returned again
    to watch her moods.

Notes

4. The Great Disappearing Act

1. Kornfield, J. (1993). *A Path with Heart: A Guide Through the Perils and Promises of Spiritual Life*. Published by Bantam. Retrieved from https://www.goodreads.com/quotes/222718-this-life-is-a-test-it-is-only-a-test-if
2. Robert Scheinfeld, "The Invisible Path to Success", Chapter 3 www.robertscheinfeld.com

5. Gascony and the Gunboat

1. Waring, L.L. (1971). *Hardings of Northumberland County, Virginia, and their related families: mini-history, homes and churches*, pp105-106. Madison WI: Self-Published.

9. A Flippin' Cold Day

1. Lennon, J. et.al. (1967). With A Little Help From My Friends. [Recorded by The Beatles]. On *Sgt. Pepper's Lonely Hearts Club Band* [Vinyl Record]. London: Parlophone.

12. Clover Dale Creek

1. Waring, L.L. (1971). *Hardings of Northumberland County, Virginia, and their related families: mini-history, homes and churches*, pp95-96. Madison WI: Self-Published.